Created by Saraya Lyons

Find more of my books on:
www.theartistryofliving.com/saraya-lyons-books

Don't forget to leave a review if you liked it! I appreciate your support.

Month:

Paycheck 1:	
Paycheck 2:	
Paycheck 3:	
Paycheck 4:	
Extra Income:	
Total:	

Bill	Due Date	Amount	✓

Budget

- Groceries:
- Housing:
- Utilities:

Notes

Notes

Goals

Bill/Expense	Due Date	Amount	

Bill/Expense	Due Date	Amount	✓

Bill/Expense	Due Date	Amount	
			○
			○
			○
			○
			○
			○
			○
			○
			○
			○
			○
			○
			○
			○
			○
			○
			○
			○
			○
			○
			○
			○
			○
			○
			○
			○
			○
			○
			○
			○
			○
			○

Bill/Expense	Due Date	Amount	

Bill/Expense	Due Date	Amount	✓

Bill/Expense	Due Date	Amount	☑

Bill/Expense	Due Date	Amount	

Bill/Expense	Due Date	Amount	

Month:

Paycheck 1:	
Paycheck 2:	
Paycheck 3:	
Paycheck 4:	
Extra Income:	
Total:	

Bill	Due Date	Amount	☑

Budget

Groceries:
Housing:
Utilities:

Notes

Notes

Goals

Bill/Expense	Due Date	Amount	✓

Bill/Expense	Due Date	Amount	

Bill/Expense	Due Date	Amount	✓

Bill/Expense	Due Date	Amount	✓
			○
			○
			○
			○
			○
			○
			○
			○
			○
			○
			○
			○
			○
			○
			○
			○
			○
			○
			○
			○
			○
			○
			○
			○
			○
			○
			○
			○
			○
			○
			○
			○
			○
			○
			○
			○

Bill/Expense	Due Date	Amount	

Bill/Expense	Due Date	Amount	✓

Bill/Expense	Due Date	Amount	✓

Bill/Expense	Due Date	Amount	✓
			○
			○
			○
			○
			○
			○
			○
			○
			○
			○
			○
			○
			○
			○
			○
			○
			○
			○
			○
			○
			○
			○
			○
			○
			○
			○
			○
			○
			○
			○
			○
			○
			○

Month:

Paycheck 1:	
Paycheck 2:	
Paycheck 3:	
Paycheck 4:	
Extra Income:	
Total:	

Budget

Groceries:

Housing:

Utilities:

Bill	Due Date	Amount	✓

Notes

Notes

Goals

Bill/Expense	Due Date	Amount	✓

Bill/Expense	Due Date	Amount	

Bill/Expense	Due Date	Amount	

Bill/Expense	Due Date	Amount	

Bill/Expense	Due Date	Amount	✓

Bill/Expense	Due Date	Amount	

Bill/Expense	Due Date	Amount	
			☐
			☐
			☐
			☐
			☐
			☐
			☐
			☐
			☐
			☐
			☐
			☐
			☐
			☐
			☐
			☐
			☐
			☐
			☐
			☐
			☐
			☐
			☐
			☐
			☐
			☐
			☐
			☐
			☐
			☐
			☐
			☐
			☐
			☐
			☐

Bill/Expense	Due Date	Amount	

Month:

Paycheck 1:	
Paycheck 2:	
Paycheck 3:	
Paycheck 4:	
Extra Income:	
Total:	

Bill	Due Date	Amount	

Budget

Groceries:

Housing:

Utilities:

Notes

Notes

Goals

Bill/Expense	Due Date	Amount	
			○
			○
			○
			○
			○
			○
			○
			○
			○
			○
			○
			○
			○
			○
			○
			○
			○
			○
			○
			○
			○
			○
			○
			○
			○
			○
			○
			○
			○
			○
			○
			○

Bill/Expense	Due Date	Amount	✓

Bill/Expense	Due Date	Amount	✓

Bill/Expense	Due Date	Amount	✓
			○
			○
			○
			○
			○
			○
			○
			○
			○
			○
			○
			○
			○
			○
			○
			○
			○
			○
			○
			○
			○
			○
			○
			○
			○
			○
			○
			○
			○
			○
			○
			○
			○
			○
			○
			○
			○

Bill/Expense	Due Date	Amount	✓

Bill/Expense	Due Date	Amount	✓
			○
			○
			○
			○
			○
			○
			○
			○
			○
			○
			○
			○
			○
			○
			○
			○
			○
			○
			○
			○
			○
			○
			○
			○
			○
			○
			○
			○
			○
			○
			○
			○
			○
			○

Bill/Expense	Due Date	Amount	✓

Bill/Expense	Due Date	Amount	✓
			○
			○
			○
			○
			○
			○
			○
			○
			○
			○
			○
			○
			○
			○
			○
			○
			○
			○
			○
			○
			○
			○
			○
			○
			○
			○
			○
			○
			○
			○
			○
			○
			○
			○

Month:

Paycheck 1:	
Paycheck 2:	
Paycheck 3:	
Paycheck 4:	
Extra Income:	
Total:	

Bill	Due Date	Amount	✓

Budget

Groceries:

Housing:

Utilities:

Notes

Notes

Goals

Bill/Expense	Due Date	Amount	☑

Bill/Expense	Due Date	Amount	✓
			○
			○
			○
			○
			○
			○
			○
			○
			○
			○
			○
			○
			○
			○
			○
			○
			○
			○
			○
			○
			○
			○
			○
			○
			○
			○
			○
			○
			○
			○
			○
			○
			○
			○

Bill/Expense	Due Date	Amount	✓

Bill/Expense	Due Date	Amount	

Bill/Expense	Due Date	Amount	☑

Bill/Expense	Due Date	Amount	✓

Bill/Expense	Due Date	Amount	

Bill/Expense	Due Date	Amount	

Month:

Paycheck 1:	
Paycheck 2:	
Paycheck 3:	
Paycheck 4:	
Extra Income:	
Total:	

Bill	Due Date	Amount	
			☐
			☐
			☐
			☐
			☐
			☐
			☐
			☐
			☐
			☐
			☐
			☐
			☐
			☐
			☐
			☐
			☐
			☐
			☐
			☐
			☐
			☐
			☐
			☐
			☐
			☐
			☐
			☐
			☐
			☐

Budget

Groceries:

Housing:

Utilities:

Notes

Notes

Goals

Bill/Expense	Due Date	Amount	

Bill/Expense	Due Date	Amount	✓

Bill/Expense	Due Date	Amount	✓

Bill/Expense	Due Date	Amount	✓
			○
			○
			○
			○
			○
			○
			○
			○
			○
			○
			○
			○
			○
			○
			○
			○
			○
			○
			○
			○
			○
			○
			○
			○
			○
			○
			○
			○
			○
			○
			○
			○
			○
			○

Bill/Expense	Due Date	Amount	✓

Bill/Expense	Due Date	Amount	✓

Bill/Expense	Due Date	Amount	✓

Bill/Expense	Due Date	Amount	✓
			○
			○
			○
			○
			○
			○
			○
			○
			○
			○
			○
			○
			○
			○
			○
			○
			○
			○
			○
			○
			○
			○
			○
			○
			○
			○
			○
			○
			○
			○
			○
			○
			○
			○

Month:

Paycheck 1:	
Paycheck 2:	
Paycheck 3:	
Paycheck 4:	
Extra Income:	
Total:	

Budget

Groceries:

Housing:

Utilities:

Bill	Due Date	Amount	✓

Notes

Notes

Goals

Bill/Expense	Due Date	Amount	

Bill/Expense	Due Date	Amount	✓

Bill/Expense	Due Date	Amount	
			○
			○
			○
			○
			○
			○
			○
			○
			○
			○
			○
			○
			○
			○
			○
			○
			○
			○
			○
			○
			○
			○
			○
			○
			○
			○
			○
			○
			○
			○
			○
			○

Bill/Expense	Due Date	Amount	

Bill/Expense	Due Date	Amount	☑

Bill/Expense	Due Date	Amount	✓

Bill/Expense	Due Date	Amount	
			○
			○
			○
			○
			○
			○
			○
			○
			○
			○
			○
			○
			○
			○
			○
			○
			○
			○
			○
			○
			○
			○
			○
			○
			○
			○
			○
			○
			○
			○
			○
			○

Bill/Expense	Due Date	Amount	✓
			○
			○
			○
			○
			○
			○
			○
			○
			○
			○
			○
			○
			○
			○
			○
			○
			○
			○
			○
			○
			○
			○
			○
			○
			○
			○
			○
			○
			○
			○
			○
			○
			○
			○
			○

Month:

Paycheck 1:	
Paycheck 2:	
Paycheck 3:	
Paycheck 4:	
Extra Income:	
Total:	

Bill	Due Date	Amount	

Budget

Groceries:

Housing:

Utilities:

Notes

Notes

Goals

Bill/Expense	Due Date	Amount	

Bill/Expense	Due Date	Amount	

Bill/Expense	Due Date	Amount	✓

Bill/Expense	Due Date	Amount	✓
			○
			○
			○
			○
			○
			○
			○
			○
			○
			○
			○
			○
			○
			○
			○
			○
			○
			○
			○
			○
			○
			○
			○
			○
			○
			○
			○
			○
			○
			○
			○
			○
			○

Bill/Expense	Due Date	Amount	✓

Bill/Expense	Due Date	Amount	✓

Bill/Expense	Due Date	Amount	✓

Bill/Expense	Due Date	Amount	✓

Month:

Paycheck 1:	
Paycheck 2:	
Paycheck 3:	
Paycheck 4:	
Extra Income:	
Total:	

Budget

Groceries:	
Housing:	
Utilities:	

Bill	Due Date	Amount	✓

Notes

Notes

Goals

Bill/Expense	Due Date	Amount	✓

Bill/Expense	Due Date	Amount	✓

Bill/Expense	Due Date	Amount	✓

Bill/Expense	Due Date	Amount	
			○
			○
			○
			○
			○
			○
			○
			○
			○
			○
			○
			○
			○
			○
			○
			○
			○
			○
			○
			○
			○
			○
			○
			○
			○
			○
			○
			○
			○
			○
			○
			○
			○
			○

Bill/Expense	Due Date	Amount	✓

Bill/Expense	Due Date	Amount	✓
			○
			○
			○
			○
			○
			○
			○
			○
			○
			○
			○
			○
			○
			○
			○
			○
			○
			○
			○
			○
			○
			○
			○
			○
			○
			○
			○
			○
			○
			○
			○
			○
			○
			○
			○

Bill/Expense	Due Date	Amount	✓

Bill/Expense	Due Date	Amount	✓
			○
			○
			○
			○
			○
			○
			○
			○
			○
			○
			○
			○
			○
			○
			○
			○
			○
			○
			○
			○
			○
			○
			○
			○
			○
			○
			○
			○
			○
			○
			○
			○
			○

Month:

Paycheck 1:	
Paycheck 2:	
Paycheck 3:	
Paycheck 4:	
Extra Income:	
Total:	

Bill	Due Date	Amount	✓

Budget

Groceries:

Housing:

Utilities:

Notes

Notes

Goals

Bill/Expense	Due Date	Amount	

Bill/Expense	Due Date	Amount	

Bill/Expense	Due Date	Amount	✓

Bill/Expense	Due Date	Amount	✓
			○
			○
			○
			○
			○
			○
			○
			○
			○
			○
			○
			○
			○
			○
			○
			○
			○
			○
			○
			○
			○
			○
			○
			○
			○
			○
			○
			○
			○
			○
			○
			○
			○
			○
			○

Bill/Expense	Due Date	Amount	✓
			○
			○
			○
			○
			○
			○
			○
			○
			○
			○
			○
			○
			○
			○
			○
			○
			○
			○
			○
			○
			○
			○
			○
			○
			○
			○
			○
			○
			○
			○
			○
			○
			○
			○

Bill/Expense	Due Date	Amount	
			☐
			☐
			☐
			☐
			☐
			☐
			☐
			☐
			☐
			☐
			☐
			☐
			☐
			☐
			☐
			☐
			☐
			☐
			☐
			☐
			☐
			☐
			☐
			☐
			☐
			☐
			☐
			☐
			☐
			☐
			☐
			☐
			☐
			☐

Bill/Expense	Due Date	Amount	

Bill/Expense	Due Date	Amount	✓
			○
			○
			○
			○
			○
			○
			○
			○
			○
			○
			○
			○
			○
			○
			○
			○
			○
			○
			○
			○
			○
			○
			○
			○
			○
			○
			○
			○
			○
			○
			○
			○
			○
			○
			○
			○
			○
			○

Month:

Paycheck 1:	
Paycheck 2:	
Paycheck 3:	
Paycheck 4:	
Extra Income:	
Total:	

Bill	Due Date	Amount	☐

Budget

Groceries:
Housing:
Utilities:

Notes

Notes

Goals

Bill/Expense	Due Date	Amount	✓

Bill/Expense	Due Date	Amount	✓

Bill/Expense	Due Date	Amount	

Bill/Expense	Due Date	Amount	

Bill/Expense	Due Date	Amount	✓

Bill/Expense	Due Date	Amount	✓

Bill/Expense	Due Date	Amount	✓
			○
			○
			○
			○
			○
			○
			○
			○
			○
			○
			○
			○
			○
			○
			○
			○
			○
			○
			○
			○
			○
			○
			○
			○
			○
			○
			○
			○
			○
			○
			○
			○

Bill/Expense	Due Date	Amount	

Month:

Paycheck 1:	
Paycheck 2:	
Paycheck 3:	
Paycheck 4:	
Extra Income:	
Total:	

Bill	Due Date	Amount	✓

Budget

Groceries:	
Housing:	
Utilities:	

Notes

Notes

Goals

Bill/Expense	Due Date	Amount	✓

Bill/Expense	Due Date	Amount	✓

Bill/Expense	Due Date	Amount	✓

Bill/Expense	Due Date	Amount	✓

Bill/Expense	Due Date	Amount	✓
			○
			○
			○
			○
			○
			○
			○
			○
			○
			○
			○
			○
			○
			○
			○
			○
			○
			○
			○
			○
			○
			○
			○
			○
			○
			○
			○
			○
			○
			○
			○
			○
			○
			○
			○

Bill/Expense	Due Date	Amount	✓
			○
			○
			○
			○
			○
			○
			○
			○
			○
			○
			○
			○
			○
			○
			○
			○
			○
			○
			○
			○
			○
			○
			○
			○
			○
			○
			○
			○
			○
			○
			○
			○
			○
			○
			○

Bill/Expense	Due Date	Amount	

Bill/Expense	Due Date	Amount	✓

Debt Overview

List your debt from lowest to highest

Debt Name	Min. Payment	Starting Balance
Total		

Paycheck	Debt Name	Debt Balance	Debt Name	Debt Balance	Debt Name	Debt Balance
Payday	Debt Payment	Debt Balance	Debt Payment	Debt Balance	Debt Payment	Debt Balance

Debt Snowball

Paycheck	Debt Name	Debt Balance	Debt Name	Debt Balance	Debt Name	Debt Balance
Payday	Debt Payment	Debt Balance	Debt Payment	Debt Balance	Debt Payment	Debt Balance

Debt Snowball

Paycheck	Debt Name	Debt Balance	Debt Name	Debt Balance	Debt Name	Debt Balance
Payday	Debt Payment	Debt Balance	Debt Payment	Debt Balance	Debt Payment	Debt Balance

Debt Snowball

Paycheck	Debt Name	Debt Balance	Debt Name	Debt Balance	Debt Name	Debt Balance
Payday	Debt Payment	Debt Balance	Debt Payment	Debt Balance	Debt Payment	Debt Balance

Debt Snowball

Paycheck	Debt Name	Debt Balance	Debt Name	Debt Balance	Debt Name	Debt Balance
Payday	Debt Payment	Debt Balance	Debt Payment	Debt Balance	Debt Payment	Debt Balance

Debt Snowball

Paycheck	Debt Name	Debt Balance	Debt Name	Debt Balance	Debt Name	Debt Balance
Payday	Debt Payment	Debt Balance	Debt Payment	Debt Balance	Debt Payment	Debt Balance

Debt Snowball

Paycheck	Debt Name	Debt Balance	Debt Name	Debt Balance	Debt Name	Debt Balance
Payday	Debt Payment	Debt Balance	Debt Payment	Debt Balance	Debt Payment	Debt Balance

Debt Snowball

Paycheck	Debt Name	Debt Balance	Debt Name	Debt Balance	Debt Name	Debt Balance
Payday	Debt Payment	Debt Balance	Debt Payment	Debt Balance	Debt Payment	Debt Balance

Debt Snowball

Paycheck	Debt Name	Debt Balance	Debt Name	Debt Balance	Debt Name	Debt Balance
Payday	Debt Payment	Debt Balance	Debt Payment	Debt Balance	Debt Payment	Debt Balance

Debt Snowball

Paycheck	Debt Name	Debt Balance	Debt Name	Debt Balance	Debt Name	Debt Balance
Payday	Debt Payment	Debt Balance	Debt Payment	Debt Balance	Debt Payment	Debt Balance

Debt Snowball

Paycheck	Debt Name	Debt Balance	Debt Name	Debt Balance	Debt Name	Debt Balance
Payday	Debt Payment	Debt Balance	Debt Payment	Debt Balance	Debt Payment	Debt Balance

Debt Snowball

Savings

Deposit	Date	Total

Savings

Deposit	Date	Total

Savings

Deposit	Date	Total

Savings

Deposit	Date	Total

Savings

Deposit	Date	Total

Savings

Deposit	Date	Total

Savings

Deposit	Date	Total

Savings

Deposit	Date	Total

Savings

Deposit	Date	Total

Savings

Deposit	Date	Total

Savings 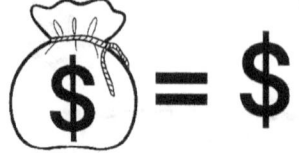 = $

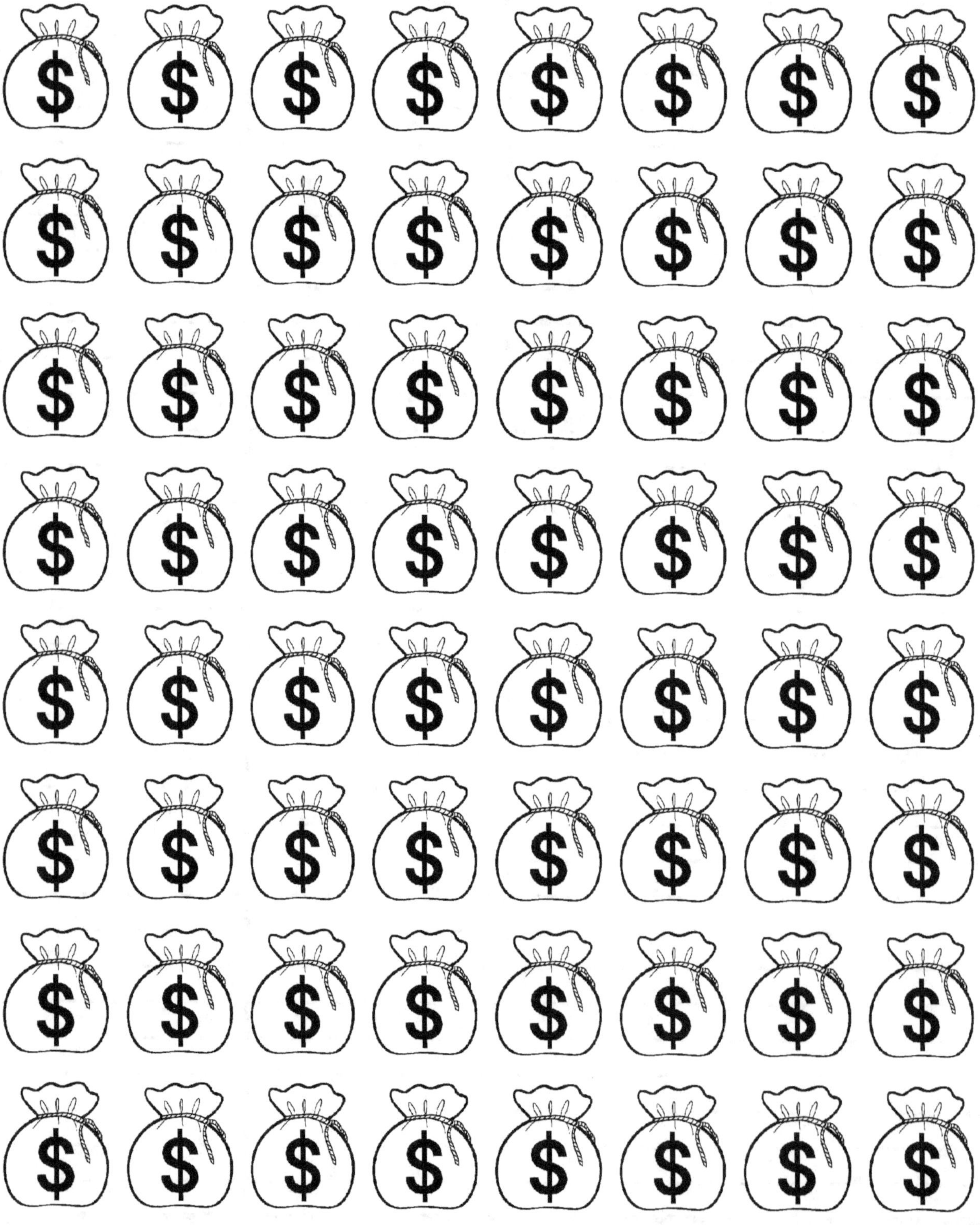

Savings  = $

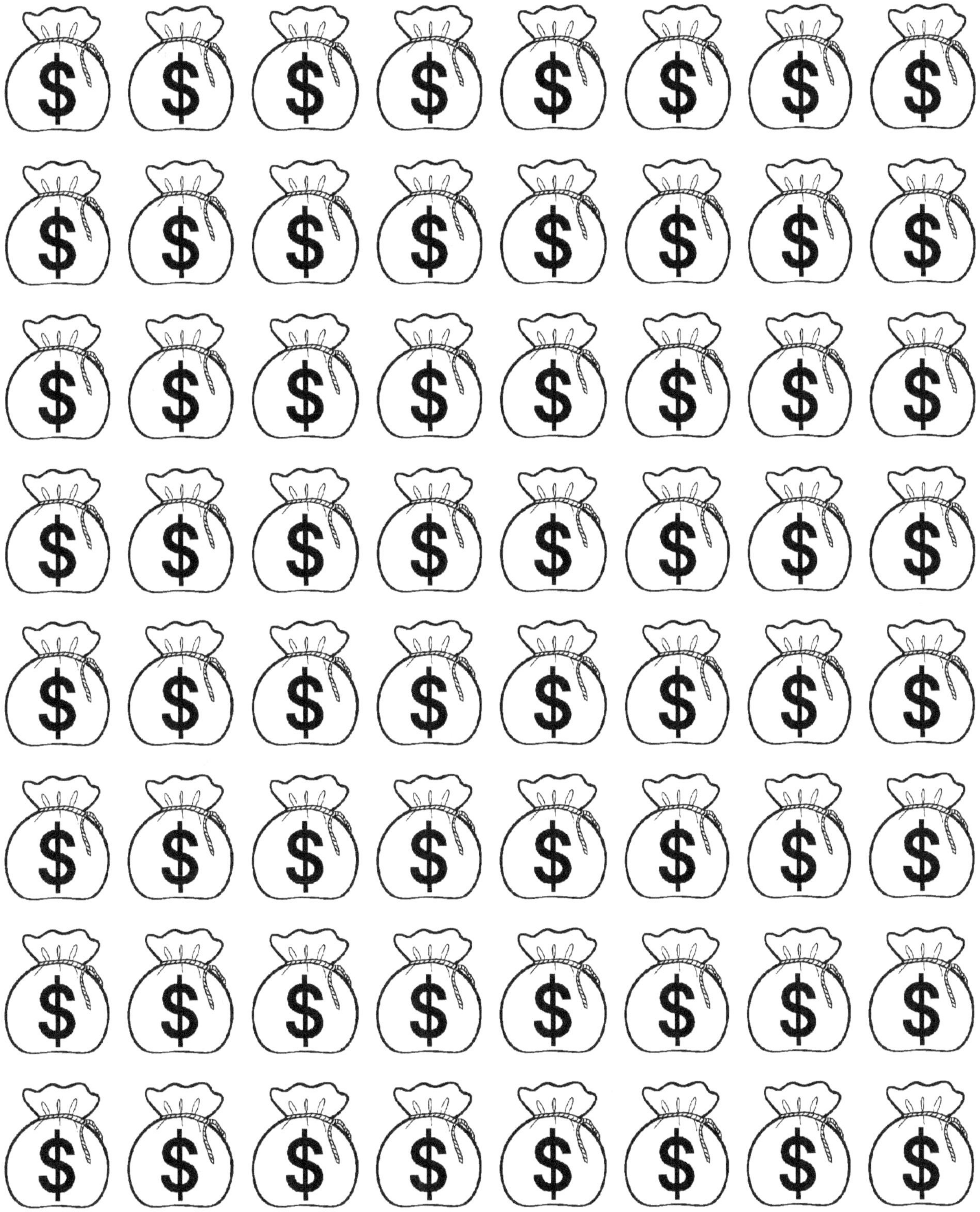

Savings 🪙 = $

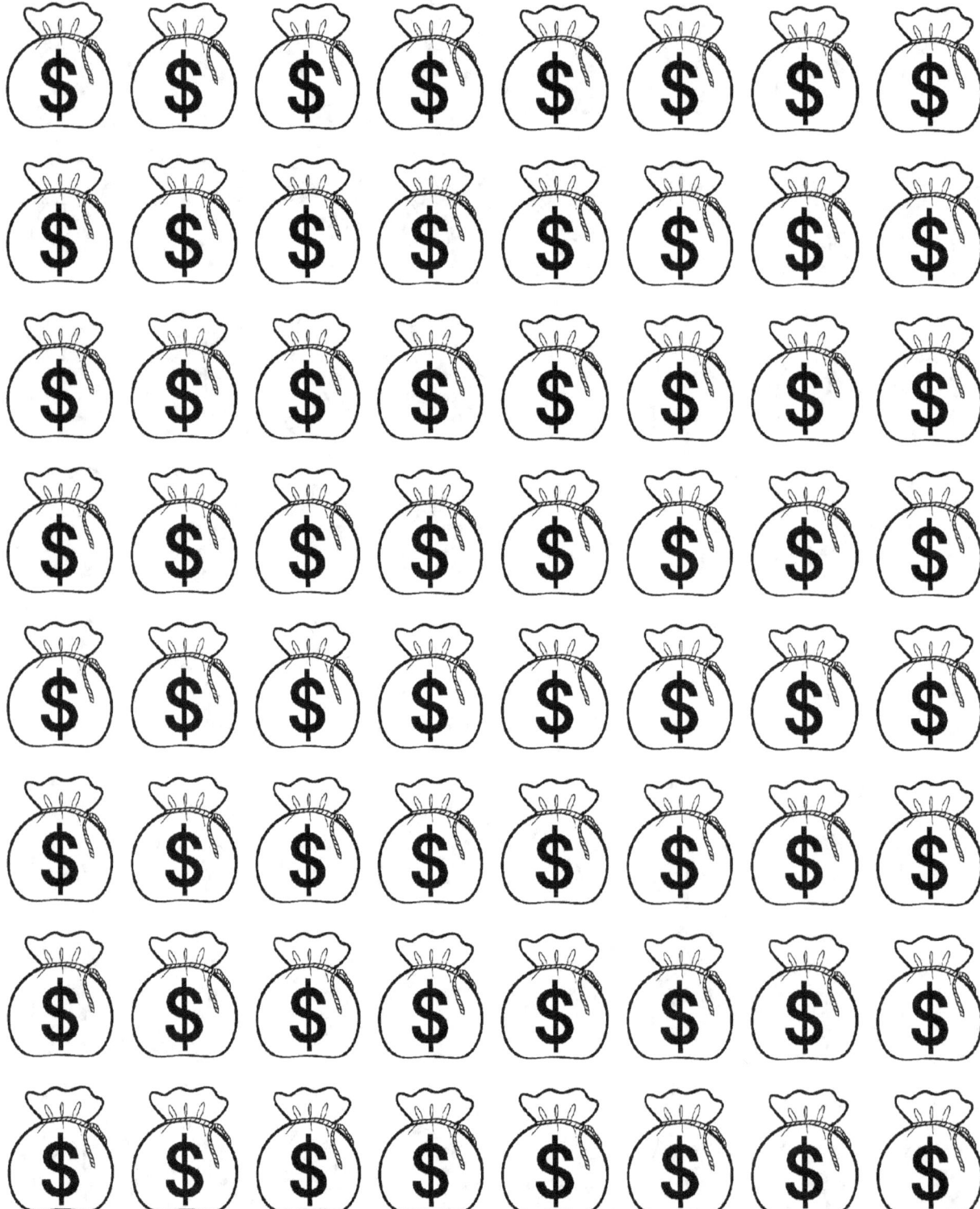

Savings 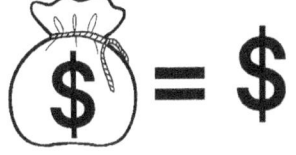 = $

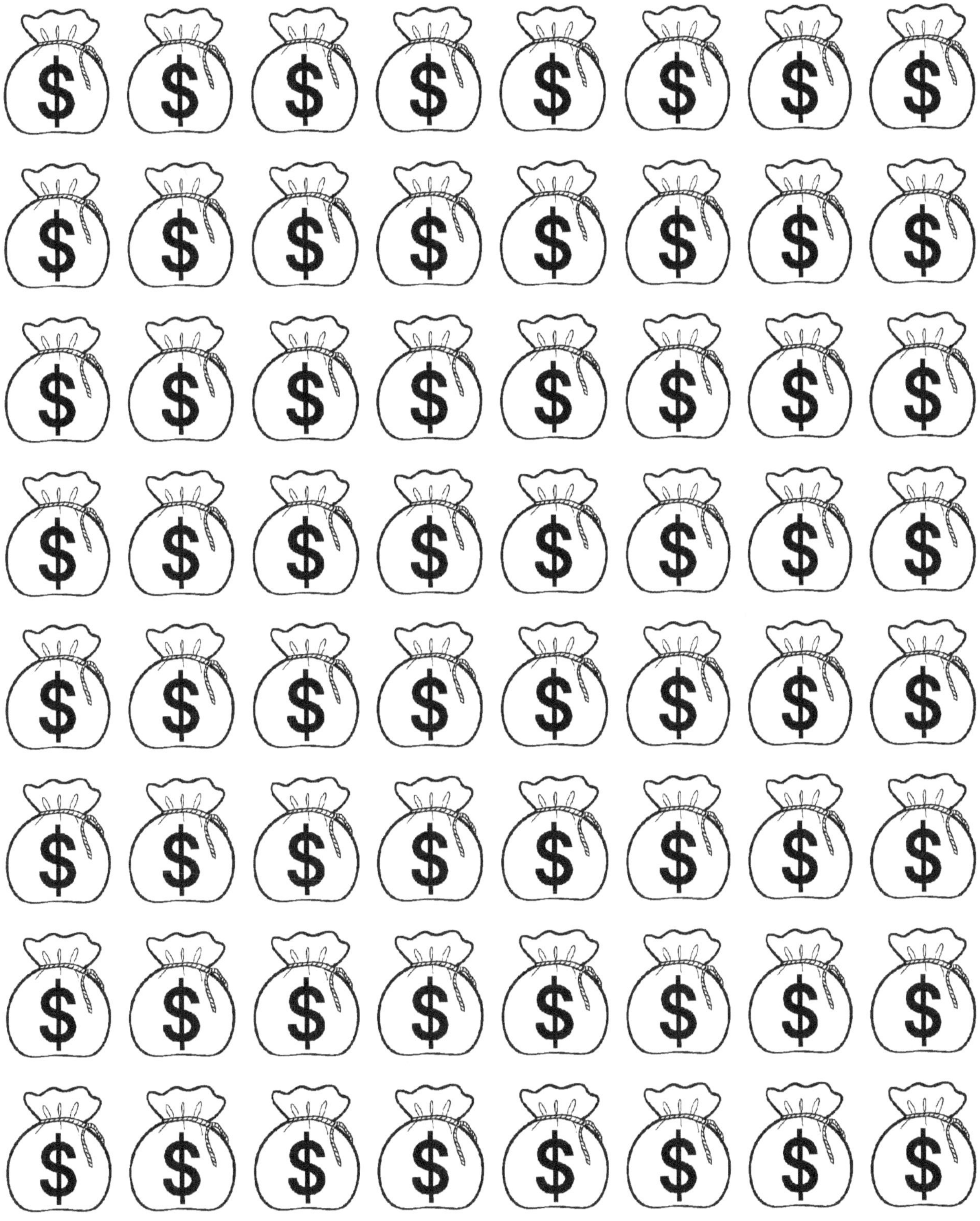

Savings  = $

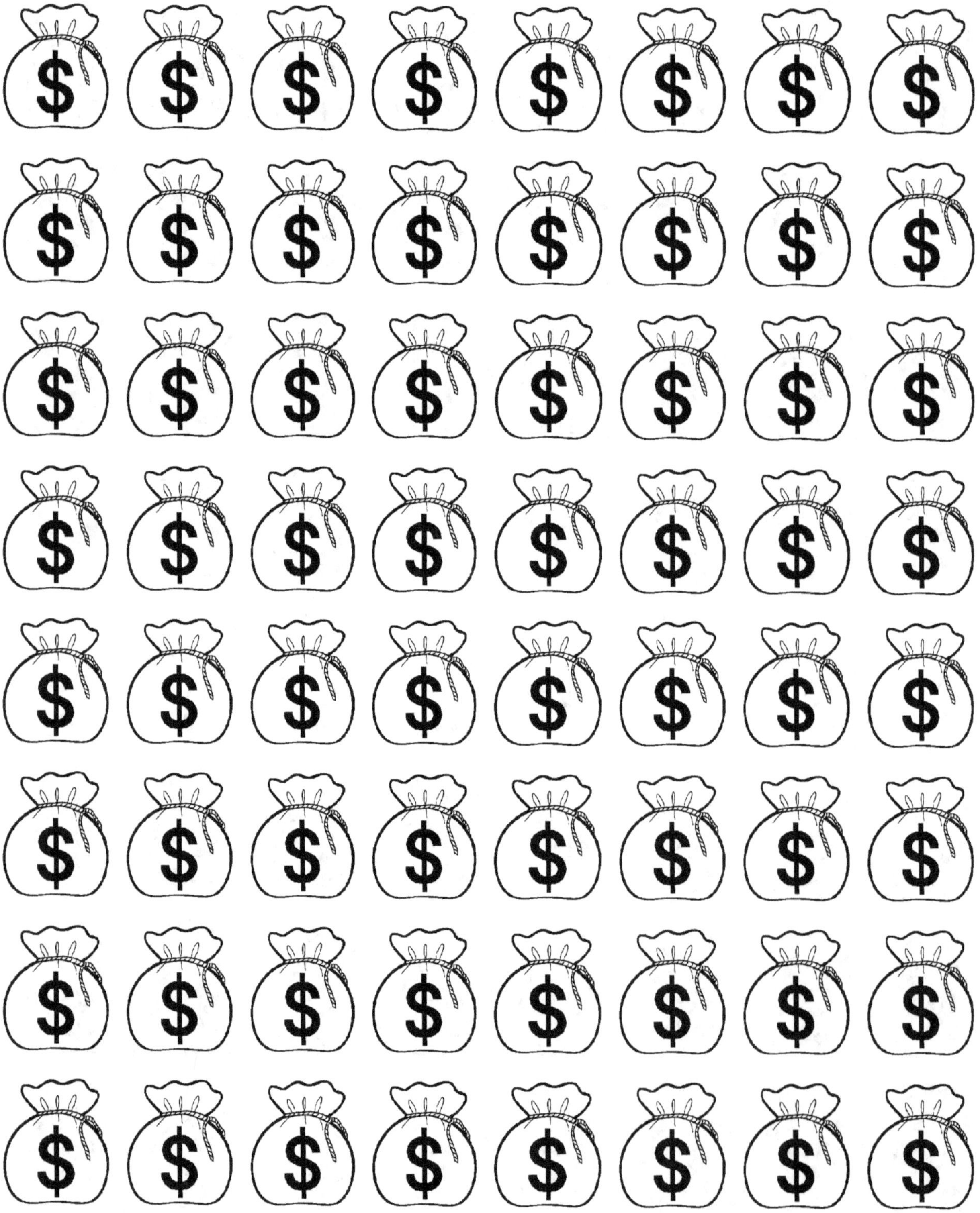

Savings 🛍️$ = $

Savings 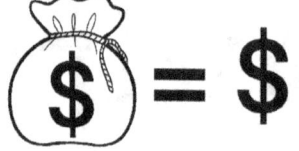 = $

Savings 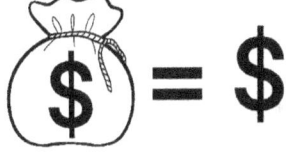 = $

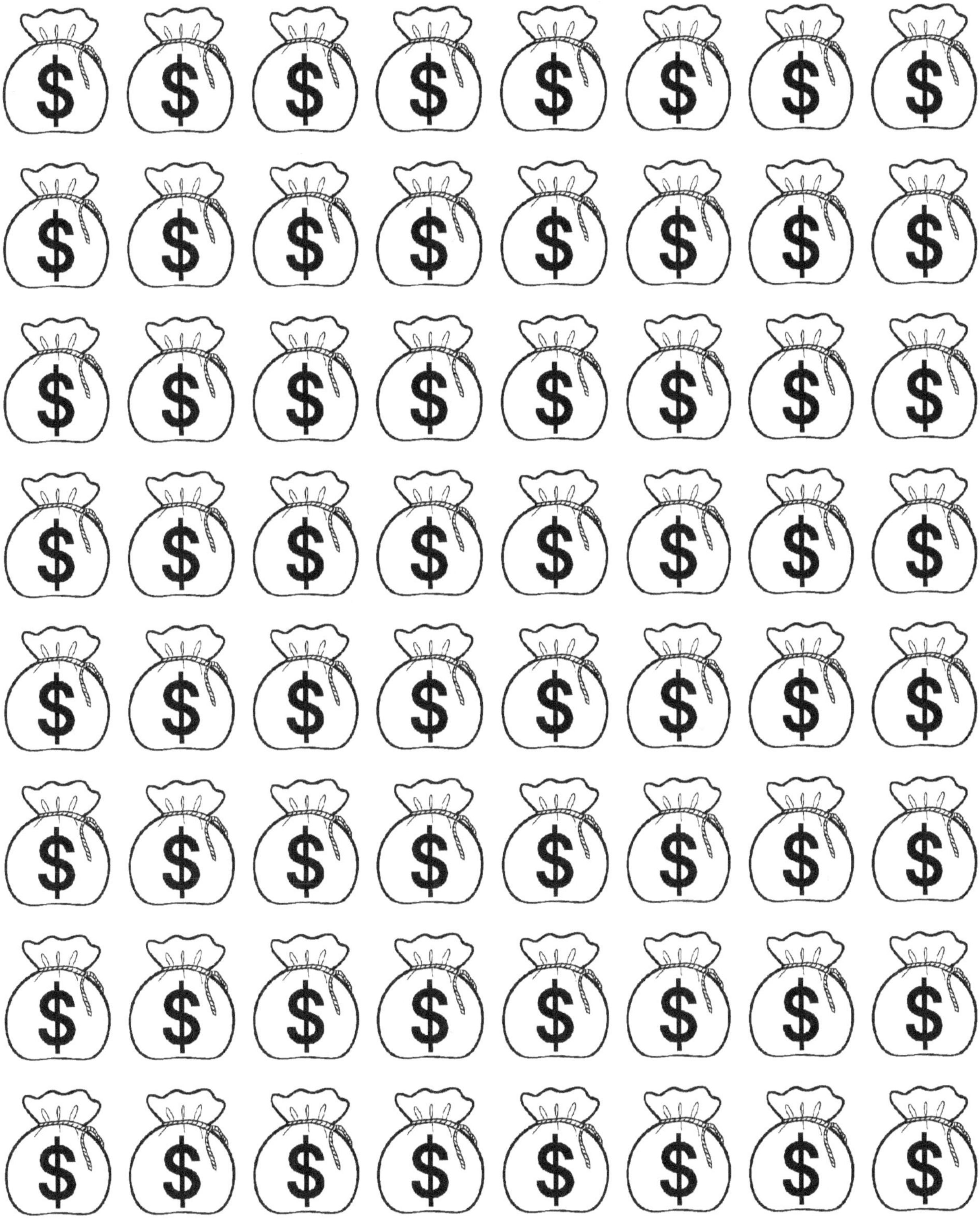

Savings 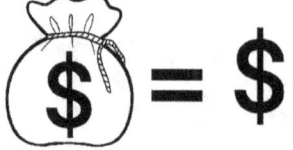 = $

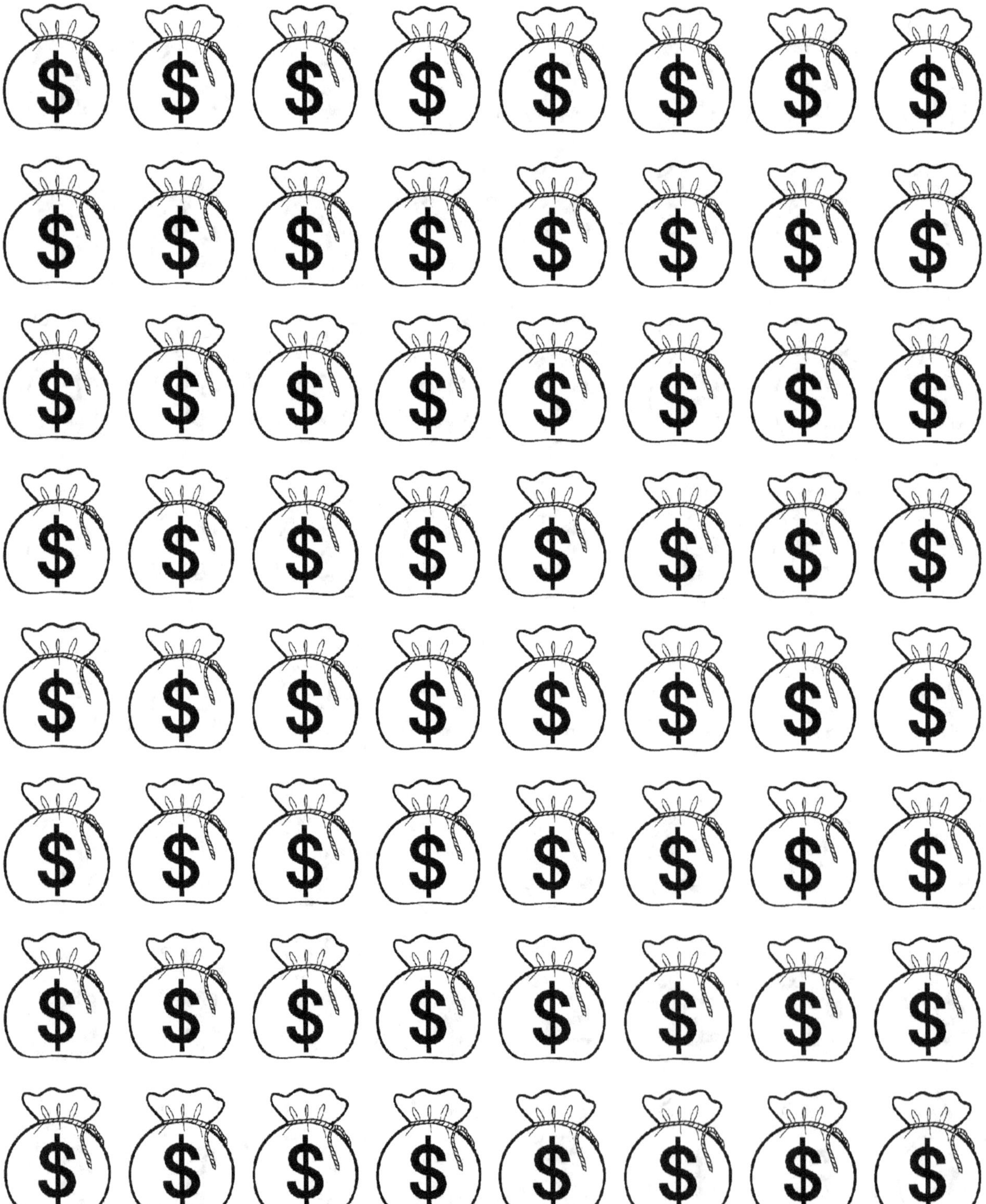

Savings    = $

www.ingramcontent.com/pod-product-compliance
Lightning Source LLC
Chambersburg PA
CBHW081430220526
45466CB00008B/2332